AUSSIE
SLANG

A POCKET GUIDE TO
AUSSIE
WORDS & PHRASES

So you don't look stupid
when trying to understand
the Australian accent

PREFACE

Australia is home to the Australian accent but for people from outside the continent, the dialect may sound friendly but foreign.

This mini illustrated 'dictionary' of Australian colloquial words, sayings and explanations is here to rescue you.

BLOODY OATH!

ACCA DACCA

The band AC DC.

"Nathan's favourite band is Acca Dacca."

ACE

Excellent.

"Nathan bought some new trainers. They're ace."

ADAM'S ALE

Water.

"I paid more for Adam's Ale than I did for a beer."

AERIAL PING-PONG

Australian Rules Football.
Usually used by non-followers.

"Aerial ping-pong is not football."

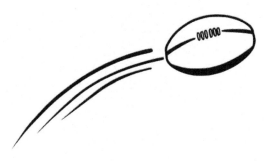

AGGRO

Bad tempered or aggressive.

"Emma is being aggro with Nathan."

ALF

A stupid person.

"Emma is aggro because Nathan is an Alf."

AMBER FLUID

Beer.

> *"Nathan has been on the amber fluid since this afternoon."*

AMBO

Paramedic.

"*The ambo said it was only heartburn.*"

ANCHORS

Brakes.

"I had to slam on the anchors because of a kangaroo."

ANKLE BITER

A child.

"Isn't she adorable, my little ankle biter."

ARVO

Afternoon.

"Emma is coming round this arvo mate."

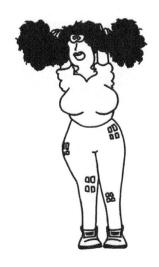

AUSSIE

Australian.

"Something tells me that arm belongs to an Aussie."

AVO

Avocado.

"This avo is so ripe and tasty."

BAIL

To cancel plans.

"Nathan has bailed on us again to go shopping with Emma."

BANANA BENDER

Someone from Queensland.

"Banana benders are a smiling bunch."

BANANALAND

Queensland.

"Bananaland is known as the sunshine state."

BARBIE

Barbeque.

"Fire up the barbie mate, I'm craving a sausage'."

BATHERS

Bathing suit, used mostly in
Western Australia.

"See Nathan, my bathers fit perfect."

BEAUT

Great.

"That was a beaut little dessert."

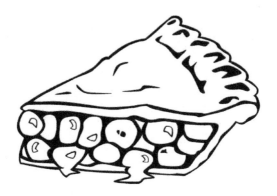

BEVVY

A beverage, usually a cold beer.

"Have a bevvy mate."

BIFF

Fight.

"Nathan got into a bit of a biff after a bevvy."

BIG BIKKIES

Expensive.

"Nathan bought a TV that cost big bikkies but it looks like a microwave."

BIKKIE

Biscuit.

"This bikkie didn't cost big bikkies."

BITIES

Biting insects such as
mosquitoes and midges.

*"These bities are going to start on my
bikkies after they've finished with me."*

BIZZO

Business.

"Mind your own bizzo Nathan."

BLOODY OATH

A term of agreement.

"Bloody oath this really is the best dish I've ever tasted."

BLUDGER

A lazy person.

"Nathan is the most accomplished bludger I know."

BOOMER

A male adult kangaroo. OR something large.

"Boomers know how to fight in the wild."

BONZA

Great, excellent.

"That was a bonza hike yesterday."

BORRIE

Regional slang for shit.

"Nathan has gone for a borrie."

BOTTLE-O

Off-license, liquor store.

"Just swinging by the bottle-o before I go home."

BRISVEGAS

The city of Brisbane.

"We're going to Brisvegas for the weekend."

CACTUS

Dead or broken.

"We didn't go to Brisvegas, the car was cactus."

CHOKKIE

Chocolate.

"No chokkie for me, I'm on a diet."

CLACKER

Anus.

"Get out of the way Nathan, all I can see is your clacker."

COLD ONE

A beer.

"Have a cold one mate."

COSSIE

Swimming costume.

"I'll put my cossie on and have a cold one in the pool."

CRIKEY

An expression of surprise.

"Crikey! He will be getting a speeding fine."

COCKI

A cockroach.

"That cocki looks big on paper."

DAKS

Trousers.

"Mum, I need my daks washing."

DATE

Bum.

"Get off your date and wash them yourself Nathan."

DATE ROLL

Toilet paper.

"Nathan! You've finished the date roll."

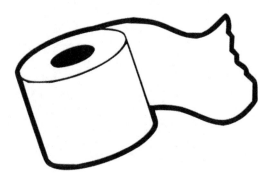

DIGGER

Soldier.

"When I grow up I want to be a digger."

DILL

An idiot.

"Nathan wants to be a digger. The dill."

DINKUM

True, genuine.

"Are you fair dinkum about your bad back?"

DINKY DI

Legitimate, the real deal.

"Do you think he's a dinky di Aussie?"

DRONGO

An idiot.

"Don't tell me you forgot to put the beer in the fridge you drongo."

DUNNY

Toilet.

"You've been in the dunny for 45 minutes now Nathan."

DUNNY
BRUSH

Toilet brush.

> *"And make use of the dunny brush when you're finished."*

ESKI

Plastic insulated cooler box for
food and drinks.

"The drinks are in the Eski."

FAIR GO

A chance.

"Emma you didn't even give me a fair
go at telling you why I was late."

FAIRY FLOSS

Candy floss.

"Am I too old for fairy floss?"

GABBA

Brisbane Cricket Ground.

"It will be a beaut day at the Gabba."

GALAH

Idiot.

"Nathan you're a flaming galah."

G'DAY

Good day. Hello.

"G'day mate."

GROG

Alcohol.

"Need some grog after that stereotypial 'g'day mate' greeting."

HEAPS

Lots.

"After heaps of studying, Emma did heaps of sleeping."

ICY POLE

An ice lolly.

"Emma needs an icy pole to wake her up in this heat."

JUG

An electric kettle.

"The jug has just boiled for your coffee now that you've had your icy pole."

KIWI

A person from New Zealand.

"Nathan was mistaken for a Kiwi."

LOLLIES

Sweets (candy).

"Nathan you're 28, you no longer have to ask your mother for lollies."

MACCAS

McDonalds.

"Bloody oath! Forget the lollies. They have 5 buck nuggets at Maccas."

MANCHESTER

Bedsheets and linen. Not the place in England.

"Where's the Manchester isle?"

MATE

The go-to term of address for anyone.

"I don't know you mate but g'day mate."

MCG

Melbourne Cricket Ground.

"I have tickets to watch the final at the MCG."

MILKO

Milkman.

"The new milko is here with the freshest milk."

NAH YEAH

Yes. It does not mean no.

"Are you in charge in your relationship with Emma?"
"Nah yeah."

OUTBACK

Anywhere that is remote and arid.

"I hope I get signal in the outback."

OZ

Australia.

"The land of Oz mate."

PARRO

Completely drunk.

"Let's get parro after work."

PISS

Beer.

"Have you bought the piss yet Nathan?"

PLUGGER

Flip flops / thongs.

"I've busted my plugger, can I have a pair of yours?"

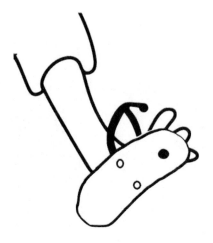

RACK OFF

Go away, get lost.

"Rack off Nathan, you're not having my pluggers."

RELLIES

Relative.

"The rellies are coming over tonight."

RIPPER

Fantastic.

"Emma's a bloody ripper mate."

ROO

Kangaroo.

"A male roo doesn't have a pouch. I bet you didn't know that."

SCORCHER

A very hot day.

"Bloody scorcher today mate."

SERVO

Petrol/gas station.

"The servo is 125km away."

SHEILA

A woman.

"Is that a sheila?"

SHE'LL BE APPLES

It will be OK.

"I know Emma was being aggro but she'll be apples mate."

SHOVE OFF

Go away.

"Just shove off Nathan."

STREWTH

An expression of surprise.

"Are they yours? Strewth!"

SUNBAKE

Sunbathe to get a tan.

"Emma is at the beach to sunbake."

THONGS

Flip flops.

"Your thongs bring out the colour in your eyes."

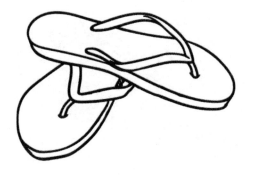

TOGS

Swimsuit.

"These are my togs, it's not my cossie."

UP SHIT CREEK

Knee deep in a problem.

"You'll be up shit creek if Emma finds out you're talking about thongs with other girls."

UTE

Small utility truck.

*"Grab the ute mate. Let's pick up
Nathan from up shit creek."*

WHITE
POINTERS

A topless sunbathing woman.

"Mate! Stop the Ute! White pointers on the beach 7 o'clock position."

YABBY

Australian crayfish.

"I did fancy a yabby for dinner but that one is way too cute."

YAKKA

Work.

"Sitting at your computer is seriously hard yakka."

YEAH NAH

No.

"Do you love Emma?"
"Yeah nah."

YOBBO

A male, loud-mouthed youth.

"That yobbo next door is arguing again."

SHOVE OFF
SHOVE OFF
SHOVE OFF
SHOVE OFF
SHOVE OFF
SHOVE OFF
SHOVE OFF
SHOVE OFF
SHOVE OFF